DISCOVERING THE ESSEX COAST

DISCOVERING THE ESSEX COAST

A brief guide to the popular resorts
and some nearby places of
historic interest

by RUDOLPH ROBERT

Published by

ESSEX COUNTRYSIDE

LETCHWORTH PRINTERS LTD., NORTON WAY NORTH

LETCHWORTH, HERTS

By the same author

HISTORIC HERTFORDSHIRE

Printed by Letchworth Printers Ltd., Norton Way North, Letchworth, Herts.

CONTENTS

LIST OF ILLUSTRATIONS

FOREWORD

Plus ca change

OUR way of life in the past fifty years has undergone changes without parallel in history. Innovations have been swift and breath-taking, but there is at least one great institution that remains very much the same as early in the century—the English seaside holiday.

It is not exactly the same, of course, because the wheel of progress has turned so fast that even the remote countryside bears the imprint of modernization—witness the motor-cars crowding every village street, the marching pylons, the jet aircraft and the television aerials. Gas lamps have been replaced by electric light, trams by buses, the black-and-white silent films by colour talkies, and so on.

Yet, as the French say, *plus ça change, plus c'est la même chose*. People, despite their higher incomes, their wider freedom of action and their greater sophistication, still retain a taste for the simpler pleasures of life. The modern " gimmickry " no doubt has its appeal, but basically it is the promenades and piers, the sands, the incoming tides, the fishing boats, the yachts and dinghies, the rusting anchors, the lobster pots and coils of rope, that are the abiding attraction.

Holiday-makers in Essex have reason to consider themselves fortunate. The principal resorts have advanced with the times, and most have in recent years acquired a distinctly " new look." Whatever may be needed to make a short vacation enjoyable the Essex resorts will have it—from palatial hotels to bed-and-breakfast boarding houses, from French wines to draught beer, from wedding cake to candyfloss. Great efforts have indeed been made by the civic fathers to be "with it," to lay on space-age effects, and in general to follow the contemporary trend. Nevertheless, the resorts, especially those farthest from London, are still comparatively unspoilt. Inland the visitor will find a pleasant and uniquely historic countryside.

With its various indentations, the Essex coastline is of considerable length. Where along the course of the muddy Thames does it actually begin? Tilbury and Canvey Island, which may occur to mind, are both too much within the estuary to be seriously considered. For present purposes, therefore, the starting point is held to be the place that formerly marked the limit of London's authority over the river, and rose to fame early in the nineteenth century after two members of the royal family—the infant Princess Charlotte and her mother, Princess Caroline of Brunswick—had spent holidays there. The place referred to is easily guessed. Everyone knows it, everyone has been there, for it now stands in much the same relation to the south of England as Blackpool does to the north.

Chapter I

SOUTHEND-ON-SEA

THIS is not, perhaps, one of the most happily situated seaside resorts. It has a reputation for mud and capricious tides; the surrounding countryside is flat and undistinguished. One is aware all the time of the close proximity of London and of the warehouses, power stations and oil refineries that flank the sluggish estuary.

Yet every year during the summer months Southend-on-Sea is visited by tens of thousands of excursionists who come by train, steamer, car, coach and motor-cycle from London, from towns and villages in the Home Counties, and from even more distant places. Whole families, including grandparents and infants, are impelled to make this migration despite the inconvenience of travel, the vagaries of the weather and the certainty of madding crowds when their destination is reached. What is it that attracts them? What do they hope to experience in their few hectic hours by the sea?

Mainly, one imagines, the object is to escape an all-too-familiar environment; to exchange the sight of bricks and mortar for a refreshing glimpse of sand and sea. People—even the most industrious—must have an occasional break from the routine of factory, office or household; and for the East Londoner, as for many Essex and Hertfordshire folk, there is a certain inevitability about the choice of Southend—which they know, which has such profusion of amusements, and is so near. Certainly one could go farther and fare worse, for Southend, granted a sunny day and a full tide, can be quite enchanting.

Entertainments

Though there is little scenically to beguile the eye in Southend, it must be admitted that the cliffs and gardens, with their zigzagging paths, are in every way delightful. At the top, and on the way up, will be found many excellent vantage points from which to stand and stare—at the panorama of cloud and sea, at the yachts and dinghies in the water offshore and at the big ships far out. It is, indeed, just as possible to spend a contemplative half-hour in the cliff gardens and parks of Southend-on-Sea as in those of many a more pretentious place. However, people do not go to Southend for the views; usually the intention is " to have a good time," which implies activity and getting down to the esplanades and beaches.

As most people will know, Southend has not just one sea-front, but several. The promenades that link Leigh, Westcliff-on-Sea, Southend, Thorpe Bay and Shoeburyness are, in fact, seven miles long. The busiest section is that near the pier entrances. Here, on Western Esplanade and Marine Parade, are situated the boating and swimming pools, the children's playgrounds, and the amusements and entertainments for which the hordes of holiday-makers have come and for which they are avid. Though every taste is catered for, the fun and games tend to be of the more robust kind. For a shilling or two it is possible to look over a replica (or what is claimed to be a replica) of Sir Francis Drake's *Golden Hind* and see the Spanish Inquisition at its grisly work; another small outlay gains admittance to a waxworks with a special display of malefactors being boiled in oil, of hangings, drawings and quarterings, and of unfortunates dying the death of a thousand cuts. Here too are gambling machines, racing games, distorting mirrors, dodgem cars, and places in which bingo is played in an atmosphere of rapt concentration. The Kursaal, with its amusements, cocktail bars and ballroom, is for many people a full day's entertainment in itself.

Cockles, whelks, oysters

Eating and drinking are important to the holiday-maker, for unaccustomed exercise and sea breezes combine to sharpen appetite and provoke thirst. Southend, it must be admitted, does its best to allay both. Apart from the restaurants and hotels in which the tycoons, with their womenfolk, partake of *pâté de foie gras* and champagne, countless establishments exist for the benefit of the day tripper, who knows what he likes but is not too fussy about a gravy stain on the tablecloth. " Roast beef and two veg " or " fried plaice and chips " and " a pot of tea for two " are the staple commodities that help to keep body and soul together.

For the occasional snack there are the local delicacies to choose from: cockles, whelks and oysters, eaten standing up at a booth, or, if you prefer them, shrimps, prawns or lobster, washed down by a lemonade or a glass of beer at the nearest pub. Then on to ice-cream, a bagful of plums or cherries—and potato crisps!

The pier

As we have said, Southend has no striking scenic features, yet there is one man-made object that dominates everything and can hardly be ignored—the pier. Approximately one and a quarter miles long, it is to Southend very much what the Eiffel Tower is to Paris or the Empire State Building to

New York—a wonder of the world, something at which to gape in awe and incredulity. For sixpence you can buy a booklet published by the borough authorities, and read about its history (which begins in 1828)—how it came to be built, how much money has been invested in it, and how huge a success it has been. Electric trains are there to take you in comfort across the mud flats to the end.

There, with the waves murmuring below decks and the gulls screeching overhead, is indeed a little paradise. Though safely linked to *terra firma*, one enjoys the illusion of being on a luxury liner, of *Queen Mary* proportions, steaming through stormless oceans in search of freedom and the sun. True, the liner is a little overcrowded with passengers; the sun-worshippers are out in force, and it is only with difficulty that newcomers can find a seat. Some drift off to the concert hall, to the amusements, or to the life-boat house. Those who have come prepared with rod and line settle down hopefully, with their eyes fixed on foam-flecked waters and bobbing floats. In the sea at the end of the longest pier in the world are plaice, dabs, eels, flounders, herrings and many other species of fish, and angling is encouraged.

The secret

What else is there about Southend to lure young and old within its bounds? One thinks of trips aboard the *Skylark*, swimming, the carnival processions, the streets full of souvenir shops, beauty parades, cosy tea parlours, ice-cream bars—and the picture postcards. There are, too, the speedboats, Prittlewell Priory, Southchurch Hall, Queen Victoria's statue, Punch and Judy and—lest we forget—the illuminations, which every night from August to October transform Southend and Westcliff into a veritable fairy-

Southend-on-Sea. The English weather is as fickle as ever it was, but when it is nice it is very, very nice.

Southend-on-Sea. The Palace hotel (formerly the Metropole) was patronized by fashionable society and the well-to-do middle class in Edwardian days. In 1961 it ceased to be an hotel and was converted into flats for the retired.

Southend-on-Sea. The same hotels, the same furnished apartments, the same amusements—but much more highly mechanized, more ingenious and fascinating.

Only a short walk from Pier Hill are these delightful old houses, reminding us of the days when Southend was patronized by royalty and the London quality.

Southend-on-Sea. Queen Victoria's statue occupies a prominent position opposite Clifftown Parade, amid flower beds and trees. The statue was presented to the town by Bernard Tollhurst, an ex-mayor, and was produced in the Rome studios of J. W. Swynnerton. It was erected in 1897 (but on another site) on the occasion of the queen's diamond jubilee. The statue and pedestal, of Carrara marble, have an overall height of twenty feet. The queen, seated on a Gothic chair, holds the royal sceptre in her left hand and with her right points out to sea.

Prittlewell Priory, which is now a museum, was founded about 1100 by Robert, the son of Sweyn, and functioned as an ecclesiastical institution until suppressed 400 years later. Situated in a well-timbered park only a short distance from the centre of Southend-on-Sea, the priory is well worth a visit. Among the picturesque ruins is a beautiful garden.

Church Hill steps at Leigh-on-Sea.

The " Golden Hind " at Southend-on-Sea—a replica of the ship in which Drake circumnavigated the globe.

Leigh-on-Sea. Boats on the foreshore at low tide.

Old cottages at Leigh.

Prittlewell Priory. The cross, a conspicuous feature of the cloister garth, is in memory of the Cluniac monks. Nearby is a delightful old-world garden.

land. They in themselves attract 2,000,000 visitors annually, from home and abroad.

The secret of Southend's popularity is not really hard to find. It is breezy, it is homely, it is healthy. Southend has something for everyone, and is obviously concerned that people should enjoy themselves, whether they come as millionaires with limitless time and money at their disposal or merely as day trippers let loose for a few hours of hard-earned and rowdy pleasure. Caviare or jellied eels, it makes no difference to Southend, which extends a hearty welcome to one and all.

Southend, it may be added, has a number of interesting literary associations. Among its best-known authors are Sir Edwin Arnold the poet, Warwick Deeping the novelist, and Benjamin Disraeli who was both novelist and politician. It was Disraeli who described Southend and its environs as the "Essex Riviera" and wrote to a friend "I can answer for Southend being very pretty."

Chapter II

PRITTLEWELL PRIORY

THE bus from Southend-on-Sea to Prittlewell Priory, a "must" for every visitor with even the slightest interest in Essex history, starts from a point close to the pier. Passing along busy High Street, with its many shops, it enters Victoria Street, and stops outside the park gates. Though of less than ten minutes duration, the journey is long enough to take one well away from the hectic gaieties of the town into semi-rural surroundings. The change is, in fact, quite astonishing.

Priory Park, though comparatively small, still has an air of unspoilt countryside about it. The ground undulates like a stretch of wild moorland; there are clumps of stately trees to remind us that this was once a woodland area. A tiny stream, a tributary of the Roach, trickles under rustic bridges. It is a captivating scene, particularly when the priory comes into view, and must have been even more so in the remote days just after the Norman Conquest, when the name Prittlewell first began to acquire historical significance.

The actual date of the founding of the Cluniac priory was A.D. 1100, the year in which Henry I commenced his long, and on the whole enlightened, reign. According to an old document, it was Robert the son of Sweyn, also known as Robert de Essex, who founded the priory, granting it the church of Prittlewell and "whatever the three priests of that church hold in lands and in grass and in tithes." Five shillings yearly was to be paid to the priory of St. Pancras at Lewes in Sussex, the prior of which should for ever "have the correcting, ordaining and governing of the monks of Prittlewell . . . according to the rule of St. Benedict and the Order of Cluny." It was further stipulated in the founder's grant that the prior of Prittlewell should render each year to the prior of Lewes, on the feast of St. Pancras, one silver mark as a token.

By the end of the twelfth century the wealth of Prittlewell Priory had considerably increased, though the number of monks does not appear to have risen above eighteen, and plans were made to add to the buildings. The magnificent refectory, which remains to impress us with its harmonious proportions, was completed, together with the prior's chamber, which has also survived. The church, over 200 feet long, the chapter house, the cloisters, the infirmary, the guest house and the buttery have all disappeared, apart from foundations and a few ruins. At the height of its glory Prittlewell Priory must have comprised a noble and inspiring group of buildings.

Behind its Gothic walls and stained-glass windows the monks prayed for the salvation of the founder and his kin. They farmed the surrounding land, practised the handicrafts, baked bread and brewed beer, gave alms to the poor, entertained nobility, illuminated manuscripts, and fostered the arts of music and painting. Sheltered from the world though they were, they yet led laborious, dedicated and austere lives, ministering to the needs of the community as no other institution could have done.

The dissolution

Something must, of course, be said about the Cluniac order and the way in which it was organized. Cluny, a town in the Saône-et-Loire department of France, was famous for its Benedictine abbey. The monks, who wore a loose black gown with a hood, were subject to a strict discipline, being forced to engage in manual labour as well as to meditate and read. What mainly distinguished the Cluniac monks from the Benedictines was their system of centralized control. Prittlewell, as we have seen, came under the jurisdiction of Lewes, and was required to make at least an annual token payment of one mark to the Sussex house. Lewes in turn was responsible to Cluny, which acted as the supreme controlling centre. The Benedictines were by comparison free, for they were not subject to such rigid forms of supervision. Yet it would be wrong to regard the Cluniacs as initiators of a new order; they were, in fact, merely an offshoot of the Benedictines, who had as their main aim the restoration and stricter observance of Benedictine principles.

To trace the history of Prittlewell Priory through the active 400 years of its existence as a religious house is not possible here. Those who have pored over the ancient records tell us that periods of halcyon calm and prosperity alternated with periods of turmoil and adversity. The priors came and went; there were occasional outbreaks of violence; days of plague and pestilence had to be lived through. Once, in 1318, a prior—William de Auvergnat—who believed he had been unfairly deprived of office invaded Prittlewell with an armed mob, " wasting its goods, expelling the monks, appropriating the muniments and common seal," and committing other excesses. However, despite all the vicissitudes of war, peasant revolt and internecine conflict, the priory survived—a solid monument to the enduring quality of the feudal system—well into the sixteenth century.

Not until 1536, when the religious orders were required to recognize Henry VIII as head of the English Church, was its existence ended. An inspection was carried out in that year by royal commissioners, and those houses with a yearly value of under £200—of which Prittlewell was one—were suppressed. The monks dispersed and the last prior, Thomas of Norwich, was retired on a small pension.

Subsequent history

Having terminated the ecclesiastical uses of the priory and taken it into his own hands, the king enriched himself by the simple expedient of selling it to a third party. Letters patent dated May 28, 1537, bearing the great seal of the king and evidencing the transfer to Thomas Audley, elder brother of the Lord Chancellor, are among the most fascinating of the Prittlewell museum exhibits. Ten years later Audley relinquished ownership of the priory and it was conveyed, for double the price he had paid for it, to Sir Richard Riche, and with the Riche family it remained until towards the end of the seventeenth century. Eventually the house known as The Priory which had arisen over the old foundations, together with some thirty acres of ground, was purchased by Mr. R. A. Jones and presented by him to the borough of Southend-on-Sea, on condition that certain work, including the excavation of the site of the priory church, should be carried out.

As a result of this agreement, which involved the corporation in considerable expense, many remarkable discoveries were made—notably a fine doorway dating back to the twelfth century, the prior's entrance to the refectory. This had been entirely covered over by brickwork and plaster. A number of carved stones, tiles and the remains of ancient burials were found. The cloister area was cleared, and the ground plan of the church—in accordance with the donor's wishes—laid bare. Other important operations included the restoration, and extension to its original length, of the magnificent refectory, with its fourteenth-century king-post roof. This is undoubtedly the most impressive and admired feature of the priory, which now serves the purpose of a museum—one of the best kept and most interesting in the county. To give everything it contains proper attention would take days. A whirlwind inspection of the interior architecture and of the main exhibits can, however, be carried out in less time than it takes to walk round a Southend supermarket or chain store.

Memorial cross

Outside again in the bright sunshine, the visitor may wander round the attractive park. Dedicated to public use by the Duke of York in 1924, it has many natural amenities, one of the principal being the River Prittle, which still feeds the ponds from which the monastery took its fish. Meandering footpaths, a fountain and a children's playground are other features of this pleasant park. Here, too, will be found fragments of the wall that formerly surrounded the monastery, the foundations of the priory church, and the cloister garth, in which stands a graceful stone cross bearing the inscription " In pious memory of the monks of the Cluniac Priory of S. Mary of Prittlewell. R.I.P. A.D. *c.* 1100-1536." At the foot of the cross lies the body of R. A. Jones, who presented the priory to the corporation of Southend-on-Sea and initiated the work of restoration and preservation. He was buried in the cloisters in 1925, at his own request.

Finally, we come to the monastery garden, ablaze with flowers during the summer months, and this in itself is well worth travelling far to see.

Chapter III

BYGONE LEIGH

A pretty little town stocked with lusty seamen

EVERYONE holidaying in Southend-on-Sea, even if only for a day, should make a point of going to see a nearby village with claims to be regarded as one of the most interesting on the Essex coast. Leigh—old Leigh, that is to say—owes its character almost entirely to the fact that it is a place in which mariners, shipwrights and fishermen—and perhaps one should add artists—have their being. The sea, the ships and the fish have, in fact, provided it with a living for hundreds of years.

Writing in the 1830s, the Essex historian Wright described Leigh (the name is variously spelt in old records as Lega, Legra, Lye, Lygh) as a parish extending eastward from Hadleigh to Southend, and supplying numerous pleasant walks and excursions to the visitors of that already popular watering place. He continues: "The land rises from the village to a considerable height, affording very extensive prospects and agreeable situations for [the building of] houses. In summer months the enlivening sea breezes, with the agreeable scenery, render this part of the county very healthy and pleasant. The village borders on the Thames, the houses being small and unpretentious. Besides the church, the Wesleyan Methodists have a place of worship here. There is a customs house and a small port." That description, despite the march of time, calls for little alteration.

Manor house and church

Like so many other fishing villages all round Britain, Leigh began as a cluster of houses on an outcrop of rock. Prehistoric man may have had a settlement there on the promontory overlooking the estuary. Certainly the Romans were familiar with the district, for many traces of their occupation have been found—coins at Leigh Hall Farm and elsewhere, fragments of pottery at Cliff Parade, an amphora on the muddy foreshore at low tide, and so on. After the Romans were obliged to withdraw from Britain, because of troubles at home, there came other conquerors, the Saxons and Normans, bringing with them new ways of living, new arts and handicrafts. Still, we may be sure that, economically, the village continued to depend on the twin harvests of land and sea.

Leigh, it is believed, was formerly part of Rayleigh but just before the Conquest was owned by a Saxon freeman and had, presumably, by then acquired its own separate identity. At the Domesday survey the manor belonged to Ralph Peverell, who built himself a house on top of the hill.

The church of St. Clement, whose tall tower was, and remains, a conspicuous landmark for mariners, is also on high ground. Both within the church and in the churchyard are several memorials to worthies of old Leigh—among them Richard Haddock, founder of a family that was to supply the Navy with two admirals and seven captains. William Brand, who commanded the *Revenge* at Trafalgar, and two masters of Trinity House—the corporation that controls lighthouses, licenses pilots and generally supervises navigation round the coasts—are also immortalized in the church interior. Nor must we overlook the memorial to Captain John Rogers, of H.M.S. *Unicorn*, who distinguished himself by his "magnanimous conduct" in the engagements with the Dutch in 1672. He died on November 30, 1685, aged sixty-five.

Descending from St. Clement's church by one of several precipitous routes, the village will be found rather uncomfortably squeezed between the railway line and the saltings. No one, however, with an eye for the charmingly anachronistic, the whimsical and the odd can fail to be captivated by it at first sight. On either side of the narrow main street are higgledy-piggledy groups of houses, pubs and eating places, curiousity shops and studios, wharves and warehouses, boat-yards and sail-making lofts. Dominant on the seaward side are the masts of the bawleys and cockle boats, pleasure yachts, catamarans and other small craft.

A naval base

Four hundred years ago, in 1553, several small Elizabethan ships, commanded by Sir Hugh Willoughby, were moored at the quays of Old Leigh prior to their departure for regions far beyond the Arctic Circle. Willoughby had left Deptford on May 10, and the reason for his call at Leigh was probably to enrol more men for his enterprise, to take on supplies of salt beef, ale and biscuits, or to get some last-minute repairs done.

For over twenty years English navigators had dreamed of charting a course to China, India and " lands as yet unknown " by way of a north-east passage. Henry VIII had been implored, as a matter of national prestige, to finance the exploration of that mysterious part of the world but had failed to act. Only during the brief reign of his son, Edward VI, in 1553, was an expedition equipped and sent to search for the route over the roof of Asia which the cartographers were sure existed.

After Willoughby's short stay at Leigh he sailed round

the Essex coast to Harwich, where for three weeks he lay at anchor. At last, on June 23, 1553, he set off on his voyage, and a stormy one it proved to be. Two of his ships, the *Bona Esperanza* and *Bona Confidentia*, became ice-locked, and before the winter was over he and the sixty-two men who had sailed with him were all dead. Only the third vessel, the *Edward Bonaventure*, ably piloted by Richard Chancellor, succeeded in reaching the White Sea and the shelter of a Russian port. Leaving his ship to winter near Archangel, Chancellor travelled overland to Moscow and was invited by the czar, Ivan the Terrible, to present himself at court. As a result of their meeting a " Muscovy Company " was later formed in London, to develop trade between England and Russia, and this—the first true joint-stock corporation—was very successful.

The importance of Leigh as a port during the reign of James I may be gauged from a contemporary list of merchant ships in Essex ports. No fewer than twenty-one vessels, a sizeable fleet for those days, are named in it as belonging to the village. Colchester, with twenty vessels, was a near competitor, and only Harwich, with thirty-six vessels, surpassed it. Later in the seventeenth century, when the bold and intrepid Dutch commander van Tromp tried to sweep England from the seas, Leigh acquired great strategic significance. This was recognized by Admiral Blake, who turned it into a naval base and made use of it to refit the British fleet. That the work was well done we may safely assume from the fact that in 1653 von Tromp was defeated and killed in a decisive engagement off the Dutch coast.

Pilgrim Fathers

There is a tradition that one of the most famous ships of all time, the *Mayflower*, was built at Leigh, and it may well have been so, though little direct supporting evidence is available. There is apparently a plaque in St. Mary's church, Bermondsey, which states that the *Mayflower* came from a Leigh shipyard—and certainly all the facilities were there for building a vessel of little more than 100 tons burden. However, whether we are dealing here with history or legend is difficult to say.

More firmly based is the claim that after crossing the North Sea from Delftshaven in Holland late in July 1620 the *Mayflower* made Leigh a port of call. She had on board thirty-five people, all of whom had left England some years earlier because of their dissension from the established form of religion. Settling first in Amsterdam and then in Leyden, they had been kindly treated and yet were not altogether happy in the land of their adoption. Eventually they decided to cross the Atlantic to North America, create a " New England " there, and start life afresh.

At Leigh the *Mayflower* took on various provisions, among them flour milled at Billericay, and also a contingent of Essex volunteers. Their exact number is not known, but they were probably people spurred on by ambition and the spirit of adventure rather than by a desire to escape from religious persecution. Each man had to take shares in a joint-stock company, or partnership, specially formed to finance the undertaking. Christopher Martin, a native of Billericay and leader of the group, was later appointed the *Mayflower's* governor. By the time that she sailed from Plymouth, on September 6, 1620, there were seventy-four men and twenty-eight women, a total of 102 passengers, on board. They landed safely at Plymouth, Massachusetts, three months later.

Many died soon after their arrival in the new world because of scurvy contracted during the long voyage.

Among the survivors were some of the Essex emigrants, who named their settlements after the towns and villages of the county, raised families and prospered. Little could these Pilgrim Fathers have dreamed that their descendants would one day be regarded as members of an aristocratic elite or that a society would be formed in America consisting of lineal descendants of passengers in the *Mayflower*, with the object of preserving their memory, their records, their history and all facts relating to them and their ancestors and posterity.

This General Society of Mayflower Descendants has branches in several of the American states, organizes meetings and holds a triennial congress.

Bawleys and cockle boats

The farming of oysters in Essex dates back to the time of the Romans, who consumed them in great quantities. Colchester is, of course, the most famous breeding centre today, but there was a time when Leigh also had its oyster beds. Here is what historian Wright has to say on the subject: "The inhabitants [of Leigh] are chiefly fishermen engaged in the oyster trade, which is in the management of a company, who annually provide proper vessels that go out for the spawn of the oyster, found in a jelly-like form in various places, particularly in Cancale Bay, on the French coast. The quality of this shore [the reference is to Leigh] which renders it peculiarly adapted to the breeding of oysters was accidentally discovered, nearly 150 years ago [i.e. *circa* 1686], by a person named Outing, who, taking this district on a lease, in a short time acquired an independent fortune."

A perusal of other works on Essex history makes it clear that Leigh formerly had its natural as well as artificial oyster beds. Unfortunately, as the water in the Thames estuary became more and more polluted the oysters ceased to thrive and in the 1870s their culture was abandoned. Later an attempt was made to revive the beds, but without success. The same adverse conditions that had driven salmon from the Thames proved inimical to the oysters.

The gathering of other shellfish at Leigh has, however, developed into quite an industry, and the sea has been made to yield a rich harvest of winkles, whelks, mussels and cockles. Raked up from the sands out in the estuary, they are brought home in the brown-sailed bawleys and cockle boats. From the boats they go direct to the cooking sheds, and from there are distributed to cafés, restaurants and stalls throughout the district. Some people, of course, are revolted by the very sight of whelks, mussels, winkles, and cockles. Others regard them as rare delicacies, or even as a staple diet, to be consumed—with many a flourish of the vinegar bottle and pepper pot—at frequent intervals throughout the day.

Much has been written about the Leigh bawleys and cockle boats, which are indeed one of the irresistible, free-of-charge sights of the old fishing village. Though neither elegant nor large, their comings and goings along the winding sea channels seldom fail to attract an audience. Not all who watch, however, know that these boats were involved in a great drama of World War II and once had their "crowded hour of glorious life." In 1940, when the British expeditionary force faced disaster on the flaming beaches of Dunkirk the cockle boats of Leigh formed part of the armada of "little ships" which successfully carried out the evacuation. They have, therefore, a small but permanent and honourable place not only in local but in the national history.

Chapter IV

CLACTON-ON-SEA—THE TAMARISK TOWN

Introduced by a holiday visitor, Aunt Clara (an entirely imaginary character), in a series of letters written to her sister.

A MAIDEN lady well into middle age but with a great zest for life, Aunt Clara had been persuaded to join a party of friends to take a holiday at Clacton, on the Essex coast. Every evening she wrote a letter to her sister Sibyl in St. John's Wood (as she had promised to do) recording her impressions and experiences. As will be seen from the following extracts, Aunt Clara had not been without her misgivings about Clacton, which had been described to her as a battlefield on which rival gangs of Mods and Rockers fought out their differences. But that, she soon discovered, was most unfair.

The notepaper used by Aunt Clara during her stay at Clacton is headed " Dulce Domum Guest House," beneath which she inscribes the day of the week (but no date). Each letter begins " My dear Sibyl " and ends " Your loving sister Clara," and is written in a neat round hand.

Saturday

Just a hasty line to let you know we've arrived safely after a very pleasant coach trip through the Essex countryside. The guest house really *is* only two minutes from the sea, and the proprietors, Mr. and Mrs. Smith-Jones, are the most friendly people. Immediately after lunch we went out for our first glimpse of the beach. The sun was shining, and though the sands were rather crowded my first impressions were good. I saw what I haven't seen for years—a Punch and Judy show, and enjoyed every minute of it, like a five-year-old. Clacton's esplanade has an Edwardian air about it which I like, and the sea views are glorious. The horizon swings in an unbroken arc from east to west, and the muddy North Sea, as you called it, is quite blue. Couldn't be more so at Cannes, I assure you.

After basking in a deck-chair for two hours we had a quick look at the pier amusements, which are the usual thing—apart from the scenic railway, and that, I should say, is unique. There are dodgem cars, distorting mirrors, rooms full of gambling machines, and a bathing pool. For the first time in my life I've seen people playing *bingo*—and was disappointed, because it doesn't seem such a wicked and demoralizing game after all. D'you remember playing lotto when we were kids? Well, it's nothing more or less than that!

PS. The folk here all seem very well behaved. No signs of violence or hooliganism—so far!

Sunday

First thing this morning it was again fine, so we went out early to look at the flower gardens, which are lovely, to watch the tide come in, and to listen to the Salvation Army band. There is a shrub planted all along the cliffs here, with a feathery leaf, that is new to me and to everyone else in the party.

After lunch we took the bus to Walton-on-the-Naze and made a tour of inspection, taking snaps of the beach, the sea-front and the pier. Eventually we reached the top of the Naze, where heavy black clouds had gathered. A tall tower there, someone told us, was built in 1794 by Trinity House as an observation post. It is, I should guess, about eighty feet high.

As the threatened storm blew over we had good views across the water to Dovercourt, Harwich, Felixstowe and the Kent coast. The exercise gave me a ravenous appetite and I was glad of the good dinner (roast chicken and fruit salad).

Monday

Thank you, dear, for your solicitous note. I can assure you, however, that all is well and we were definitely *not* all murdered in our beds on the first night. There was, admittedly, a lot of trouble when the Mods and Rockers came here some years ago. Our landlady, Mrs. Smith-Jones, actually saw them throwing bottles about, smashing windows and playing football with policemen's helmets! But it was an isolated affray, she says, and the town is normally very peaceful and quiet.

I spent the morning sunning myself under the sea wall, where it was almost tropically hot! Then, after lunch (roast beef), had a look over the martello tower—built while the Napoleonic wars were on—and thought it most interesting. In what used to be the surrounding moat they have laid out a charming model village and a railway with miniature trains. In the evening I went with the others to one of the several theatres in the town—the Westcliff, I think. Must be twenty years since I was last at an English seaside concert party. The comedians, unfortunately, still put over the same corny jokes, and the soubrettes sing the same sentimental songs. But I thoroughly enjoyed myself,

Leigh-on-Sea. A boat builder's yard.

2

Clacton-on-Sea pier, on which the lifeboat "Sir Godfrey Baring" is housed. The sea, so calm on a summer evening, can in winter be very rough. Offshore are treacherous sands.

Clacton-on-Sea pier. It is the only one in the country to include a scenic railway among its thrill-producing features.

The headquarters of a sailing club at Clacton-on-Sea. Even for those who know nothing about boats there is a fascination about such places.

Clacton-on-Sea. The war memorial, surrounded by flower-filled gardens.

Clacton-on-Sea. The Venetian bridge consists of a single graceful span.

St. Osyth's Priory. Romantic buildings and beautiful gardens.

On Clacton sands a Punch and Judy show holds a young audience quietly enthralled.

Clacton-on-Sea. The martello tower that stands (next to Butlin's holiday camp) practically at the water's edge. The tower was one of eleven built to repel a threatened Napoleonic invasion.

St. Osyth parish church framed by an old arch.

St. Osyth's Priory. Much of this magnificent oriel window is original.

and think you would have done so too had you been here.

PS. On the whole, I believe your fears about Clacton were quite groundless.

Tuesday

I am writing this late at night, as I've had a full day. In the morning I went off on my own, located the post office, and then had an alfresco lunch on the sea front (a small pork pie, some scones, half a pound of Victoria plums and a cup of tea). Then I sat taking the sun, absorbing ultra-violet rays, and watching the boats and steamers out at sea, which was as calm as a mill-pond. I have, incidentally, already acquired quite a tan.

Meantime the party had booked up for an afternoon coach tour. We went to Dedham, a charming village in the John Constable country. The parish church of St. Mary, I gather, is early sixteenth century and, according to our guide, a fine example of the Perpendicular style, whatever that may be. After all, most architecture is perpendicular, isn't it? Dedham church was rather gloomy inside, but I liked the flower arrangements—quite professionally done.

After seeing Flatford mill and Willy Lott's cottage, just across the border in Suffolk, we returned to Clacton via Manningtree (interesting old maltings) and Mistley, with good views at several places of the River Stour (which is pronounced to rhyme with "dour.").

To finish the day—which was perfect, with white, fleecy clouds floating about over the harvest fields—we had a walk through the amusement arcades and gave away quite a lot of money to what they call the "one-armed bandits." Finally we sat in a shelter in the memorial gardens just watching the world go by and staring at the coloured lights.

PS. The barometer has taken a sudden plunge.

Wednesday

This, I'm sorry to tell you, has been the day of the deluge! It was already raining when I woke up and had my early cup of tea—not the ordinary kind of rain that we have in London, but a torrential rain, driven by a hurricane wind and getting progressively worse as the weary hours passed. So we just sat in the lounge listening to the idle chatter of the other guests until lunch, when we made a dash for the flicks. Watching Walt Disney's " Fantasia " for about the sixth time we were cosy enough. After that we went to see " Dancing Waters "—coloured water jets twirling to the sound of music. Rather unusual, I thought, but with water already filling my shoes and dripping down my neck I just couldn't enjoy it. Outside the storm was still raging, and as the forecast is rain and still more rain I'm going to start packing. Perhaps after all you were right; I should never have come to this horrid place!

Thursday

You will hardly believe it, but I woke up this morning to find the sun shining out of a cloudless sky! The trough of depression had, according to the wireless, given way to an anti-cyclone! So after our gammon rashers and eggs we all made a dash for the sea front and took a bus to Jaywick Sands, Clacton's bungalow suburb, and on from there to St. Osyth's Priory, which, with its great gateway, was most impressive. You, with your knowledge of history, would have loved it. Never mind, dear, I'm bringing back some colour snaps. In the evening we went to the " Ocean Revue," another concert party, on the pier. The xylophonist was very good, and I liked the excerpts from " The Merry Widow "—no doubt about it, the old tunes are best.

After the concert I had a glass of sherry in the bar of the Royal Hotel—and so to bed!

Friday

This note, I'm afraid, is going to be short and sweet, because after trudging to Holland on Sea and back, to say nothing of the coach trip to Brightlingsea, I'm feeling exhausted. The walks along the water's edge are wonderful, but my legs are troubling me again. However, I had several rests and a most pleasant chat with one of the municipal gardeners. He told me, among other things, that the shrubs with the feathery leaves you see everywhere are called tamarisks and that their pink flowers make a very pretty sight in spring. While I was chatting to the gardener a harmless-looking youth with long hair and a guitar passed by. He was about the nearest thing to a Mod or Rocker that I've seen.

Will it surprise you to learn that I've decided to extend my holiday in Clacton by another week? The others are going back tomorrow, but there are still so many places I want to see—Colchester, Mersea and Tendring—that I simply couldn't resist the temptation to stay. I hope you're not working too hard.

PS. Why not drop everything and pop down? I'm sure you'd like it here.

Chapter V

ST. OSYTH'S ABBEY

The legend and the history

MODERN life is full of strains and stresses. People must work hard and at high pressure amid the deafening roar set up by machinery, motor-cars and jet aircraft. No wonder that at times they feel the overwhelming need to escape, if only for a few hours, into quiet places by the sea or in the countryside. Essex, despite the advancing tide of industrialism, has many retreats in which the cares of the world may be cast off. St. Osyth, a village near Clacton-on-Sea, with its ruined abbey, its well-tended lawns and its peacocks, is one of the most delightful.

On arrival one finds the usual collection of small shops, cottages and village characters. There is little to distinguish it from a hundred other Essex hamlets until, quite suddenly, a splendid medieval gateway swings into view—and then everything is changed. St. Osyth acquires dignity and splendour, and the desire to see what lies beyond the stately Gothic arch becomes irresistible.

Nor on passing into the magnificent grounds, heavily timbered and extending over 250 acres, is anyone likely to be disappointed. Indeed, all who are sensitive to the atmosphere created by romantic buildings and natural beauty must experience the sensation of entering another world—altogether more harmonious and restful than the one they leave behind. Here, one feels, is a place in which time is meaningless and the power of fate itself may be defied.

Martyrdom

Though today this corner of Essex is very peaceful it was not always so. Eleven hundred years ago Saxons and Danes fought strenuous battles here. The whole district was ravaged by fire and sword; blood flowed freely, and men died in fierce hand-to-hand combats for possession of the very spot, a little raised above the level of the marshes, on which the historic remains of St. Osyth's abbey now stand.

According to tradition the village—then known as Chich—and the land surrounding it were given by Sighere, king of the East Saxons, to his wife Osyth for the founding of a nunnery. The lady had at an early age taken a vow to remain a virgin throughout her life, but had been forced by her father to marry Sighere, who, like herself, was of the Christian faith. The marriage was not consummated and, Sighere being called away on some urgent affair of state, the bride effectively annulled the wedding ceremony by taking the veil. Subsequently, when the king returned and learned of the reason for this last-minute change of mind he not only agreed that she should be left free to fulfil her vow but magnanimously made her a gift of Chich and of a strip of land adjoining the sea. There she retired and founded a church, dedicated to St. Peter and St. Paul, and a nunnery.

Then, somewhere about 870, there arrived the Danish marauders—fierce, land-hungry and pagan—to plunder and destroy. With the ruthless Viking leaders Hubba and Inguar at their head, they created a terrible turmoil in the countryside. Not even the religious institutions were spared. At Chich the buildings were desecrated and looted and the nuns insulted. Many of them, after being ravished, must have shared the fate of the royal foundress of the convent, who, because she refused to repudiate her Christian faith, was beheaded.

So far the story has about it the ring of authenticity. We know that Christianity was introduced into south-eastern

England in the sixth century, and that before the end of the ninth century Danish raiders were challenging Saxon rule. St. Osyth may indeed have suffered in the way described. After the decapitation, however, we soar right out of the realm of history into that of legend. When told that the corpse immediately rose up and, with its head under its arm, walked to the church door, and further that a fountain of water gushed up from the spot on which the execution had taken place, we are naturally inclined to be sceptical. Such boldly embroidered romances were, of course, popular in medieval times and, like the early Greek folk tales, they often had a charm and a poetic plausibility well calculated to ensure their survival into future ages.

One other inevitable elaboration of the myth was that the fountain which spurted from the ground where St. Osyth was martyred had miraculous healing powers, and that its waters cured many diseases. Pilgrims then began to seek out the village from near and far.

A living force

Once again, in 1066, powerful and warlike men from across the sea invaded England's green and pleasant land. William, Duke of Normandy, after a few fierce battles, established himself as the new overlord. The savage forest laws which he instituted caused him to be hated, but he provided England with firm government, controlled the unruly barons, and ordered the great Domesday survey to be carried out. He was also, at least nominally, a Christian, and during his reign built, in addition to the Norman castles, many new abbeys and churches.

Not, however, until some fifty years after the Conquest was the Austin priory in honour of St. Osyth established.

The founder, Richard de Belmeis, Bishop of London, endowed it with the manor of Chich, together with the churches of Clacton, Southminster, Maryland and Althorne —to which Henry I later added two other churches outside the county. Somewhere in the middle of the twelfth century St. Osyth's priory became an abbey. It acquired wealth and, like other monasteries in the Middle Ages, exercised a tremendous influence on the life of the local community. At a time when even the monarch and the nobles were illiterate it kept alive the twin flames of culture and learning. At a time when there was an almost brutal disregard of the needs of the common man—the agricultural serf tied to the land—it provided elementary welfare services, for the monasteries dispensed alms, relieved the needs of the sick, comforted the dying, succoured the widows and orphans, and helped the destitute and vagrant.

The Christian Church, on which modern Britain seems to have turned its back in disillusion, was then a living force, upholding civilized standards in the face of feudal barbarism and ignorance. Its rule was enlightened and progressive, and among the monks were many men of high integrity and noble character. This perhaps is something we should weigh in the balance against the venality, cynicism and superstition that eventually brought the medieval Church into disrepute. Like all human institutions, it had its virtues and failings.

Discipline

Monasticism as a way of life did, of course, impose impossibly high standards. Those who adopted it dedicated themselves to the service of their religion under vows of obedience, poverty and chastity. The ascetic discipline, involving a virtual renunciation of the world, was rigorous and unsparing. Occasionally a monk, frustrated beyond endurance, would run away, and there were frequent minor backslidings.

An elaborate set of rules formulated by the Archbishop of Canterbury in 1303 indicates all too plainly that the abbots and monks of St. Osyth had not always emerged triumphant in their struggle against the world, the flesh and the Devil. The canons were enjoined to confine their conversations henceforth to matters concerning their vocation and to refrain from idle gossip. They were under no circumstances to go out of the convent unless accompanied by a brother canon. Their garments were all to be of the same colour and price—a sumptuary law hinting at sartorial extravagance and rivalry in the past. More frequent visits to the sick in the infirmary, greater care in keeping accounts and fewer raids on the poor-box were requested. The entertainment of guests in nearby Essex towns and villages at the expense of the monastery was expressly forbidden, even on such special occasions as a royal visit. Considerable sums of money, it would appear, had been wasted through past " prodigalities of hospitality and convivial excess." Finally there was a solemn admonition from the archbishop against the dangers of admitting women to the bakehouses and other offices.

For a while the warning seems to have had its effect, and then things fell back into the old easy-going routine. Four years later, when Bishop Baldock visited St. Osyth, he found it necessary to remind the monastery of the archbishop's orders and to urge their more diligent observance.

The dissolution

Following the suppression of St. Osyth's abbey in 1539, the land and buildings passed into the possession of Thomas

Cromwell, an autocratic tyrant who was employed by Henry VIII as his chief agent in organizing the Reformation, overthrowing the authority of the pope and upholding the divine right of kings. When in 1540, shortly after being created Earl of Essex, Cromwell was accused of treason and beheaded, St. Osyth's abbey reverted to the Crown and in 1553 was granted by Edward VI to Thomas, Lord Darcy, chamberlain of the king's household. The former monastery—the " house keeping great hospitality for the relief of divers small towns about it " and whose tall steeple was " a common mark for mariners upon the seas "—then became a private residence. Elizabeth I, it is interesting to note, was entertained there twice, in 1561 and 1579, and among the historic ruins is an oak tree said to have been planted by her.

Wright, in his *History of Essex*, published in 1836, records that the quadrangle of the monastery was then almost entire, except part of the north side " occupied by some modern apartments and two posterns." He goes on: " Entrance is by a beautiful gateway of hewn stone." The red-brick building now known as the Priory, which dates back to the time of the abbot John Vyntoner (1523-33), was then used by Frederick Nassau as a family seat. This building, immediately facing the visitor through the gateway arch, incorporates a much-admired oriel window, most of it original.

In more recent times the property was acquired by a well-known friendly society, and the house, with its beautiful surroundings and historic associations, was then put to use as a convalescent home to which members could go to recuperate after an illness. When we remember the fountain and the pilgrims who came to drink its healing waters history may be said at that point to have turned full circle.

Chapter VI

MARTELLO TOWERS

Many visitors to the Essex coast must have wondered about the origins of the martello towers that are to be seen in various places. Were they built, to quote the words of one of Sir Walter Scott's characters, "for the sole purpose of puzzling posterity," or did they serve some useful purpose in times past? The answer is, of course, that they were fortifications built during the Napoleonic wars to guard against the possibility of invasion. Altogether eleven Martello towers were built in Essex, at a cost of £225,000, and hardly had they been completed than the turn of events made them as obsolete as the dodo.

WHEN, in 1793, revolutionary France declared war on England, and Napoleon gathered an invasion army at Boulogne, a great deal of concern was felt in south-east England as to the adequacy of the coastal defences. Among the likely landing places were, first and foremost, the beaches of Kent and Sussex, but those of Essex were held to be almost equally vulnerable. Fortunately, Napoleon was obliged to cancel his plans, and people living on the coast were able to breathe freely again.

Ten years later, however, war broke out afresh, and early in the summer of 1804 Napoleon returned to Boulogne with a mighty invasion force. On that occasion he actually caused a medal to be struck and a monument to be raised in anticipation of his victory. Though he again failed to carry out his threat, the massive concentration of troops created widespread alarm in England, and the

Government took steps that, well-intentioned as they were, seem in retrospect to have been very hasty.

Vast sums of money were spent on the construction of defences that had the supreme test ever come would have been quite useless. The building of over eighty martello towers was but one of many follies committed in that troubled period.

A myth is born

Yet there was a certain logic about it all. Military men remembered an incident of February 1794, when a British naval squadron of three ships was ordered to the Mediterranean to support Corsicans who were in revolt against French rule. One of the main objectives of the British warships was a tower on Cape Mortella, which dominated their anchorage in the Gulf of San Fiorenzo. This tower, circular in shape and of solid construction, mounted only one twenty-four-pounder and two eighteen-pounder guns, yet put up an astonishingly strong resistance. Two of the British frigates bombarded the tower for several hours, but were obliged to withdraw after one of them, the *Fortitude*, had suffered heavy casualties. Over sixty of her crew were killed or wounded, and she herself was set on fire.

Fourteen hundred marines, with supporting artillery, attacked the tower by land, and they too were repulsed. Not until a lucky shot set an inflammable parapet-lining ablaze were the defenders, numbering only thirty men, obliged to surrender. Certainly it was a remarkable episode, but out of it, regrettably, sprang the myth—for it was no more—that martello towers were impregnable fortresses. Few people had the temerity to question that belief, to remonstrate, or to suggest that a better way of spending the money, and strengthening the country's defences, would have been to build more fighting ships.

Waterloo

Among those who had thought that the Napoleonic armada might strike at Essex was Sir John Moore (later to win fame as the hero of Corunna), who made a tour of the county in 1797. He was particularly concerned about Clacton beach and the excellent anchorage it provided. An army landing there, he pointed out, had only a twelve-mile march to Colchester, " where the great road to London joins."

The strange thing is that, despite the general concern, it was not until 1808 that land was purchased in Essex and the first of eleven towers begun. To what extent the plans followed the original *Tour de Mortella*, or " myrtle tower," in Corsica is uncertain, but it was of the same circular shape, and had mountings for two or three guns. Access to the interior was obtained by climbing a ladder, which could afterwards be drawn up to a door twenty feet or so above ground. Four years after the start the Essex towers were completed and, though not actually garrisoned, stood ready for any contingency that might arise.

Nothing untoward happened, however, for by that time Britain had won command of the seas, French fortunes after the Russian campaign were on the decline, and the danger of invasion had passed. At Waterloo in 1815 Napoleon suffered his greatest and final defeat on land, and the martello towers might as well never have been built.

White elephants

What followed when peace came is, inevitably, anti-climax—a descent from the heroic to the absurd. Government officials racked their brains but could find no satisfactory alternative uses for the massive stone fortresses.

After an attempt to convert them into homes for army pensioners had failed—because of the damp and the draughts—there was a move to have them demolished, and in the course of time four actually disappeared—leaving only the existing seven. Of these " F " tower, sunk into the crown of a small hill at the end of West Marine Parade, Clacton-on-Sea, is the most accessible and interesting.

Occupied throughout the nineteenth century as a private residence, it has also served as a coastguard look-out, a meteorological station, an outpost of the Essex Regiment, a museum, and finally as the town's one and only antiquity —the " white elephant " that curious holiday-makers pay their shillings to see at close range. Unfortunately, the interior of the tower is no longer a museum, and cannot be inspected.

The great attraction, especially for children, is the moat, which has been drained and converted into a pleasant garden, with lawns, flowers and shrubs. There is also a model village, comprising such diverse features as a typical Essex main street with inns and cottages, Willy Lott's cottage (made famous by the paintings of John Constable), Framlingham castle, a row of shops, a working watermill, a miniature railway, a farmhouse complete with barns and outhouses, a windmill, and an ornamental pool with water-lilies and goldfish. Model churches from which the sound of organ music or singing emerges are among the other ingenious devices.

There are no guns (the entire battery went over the cliffs in 1883), no rusting cannon-balls, no regimental flags, not even a caricature of " Boney," to suggest the purpose for which the tower was originally built 160 years ago.

Chapter VII

CLACTON'S LIFE-BOAT

Between 1878 and 1966 the Clacton life-boat answered 620 calls for aid from vessels in distress and saved 805 lives.

A HUNDRED years ago Clacton-on-Sea, now a busy town full of boarding houses, entertainments, restaurants and shops, consisted of little more than a few old manor houses or farmsteads—Coppins Hall, Crayers and Alton Park—and half a dozen newly built houses. In fact it was not until 1871 that a start was made on construction of the Royal Hotel and of the pier. Twenty years later, however, the town was firmly established and well on the way to becoming a popular seaside resort.

The Royal National Life-boat Institution decided to open a station in Clacton in 1877, at the request of local residents. In the following year, on July 10, a life-boat named the *Albert Edward* was launched from the beach—for there was then no slipway—with ceremonies that were watched by a crowd of 12,000 people. The *Albert Edward*, an open boat, was presented to the R.N.L.I. by the English Freemasons to mark the safe return home of their grand master, the Prince of Wales (later to become Edward VII), after an extended Indian tour. The life-boat house, it may be mentioned, then occupied a site in Anglefield, at the corner of Church Road, and had to be surrounded by a fence to ensure that it was not damaged by cattle.

In that position it remained until 1884, when two slipways were constructed on the pier for use by the life-boat.

A night of storm and gale

The *Albert Edward,* launched in the pre-petrol-motor era, was little more than a suitably equipped rowing and sailing boat. As such she had many limitations, for even in comparatively calm weather the crew might be kept at sea for long periods battling against changing winds and tides. The strains and discomforts experienced in winter gales, when the *Albert Edward* was half swamped with water and her rigging stiff with ice, must have been incredibly severe. On one occasion, in January 1884, while on service in a north-west gale, the boat capsized and two of her crew of twelve—James Cross, the second coxswain, and T. Cattermole, one of the men—were lost. Both were married and had families to support.

After that tragedy Clacton's first life-boat was withdrawn from service, but a second, also presented by the Freemasons and named *Albert Edward II,* at once took her place. Between 1885 and 1901 she answered innumerable calls from ships in distress on the Gunfleet, Maplin, Buxey and other local sands. A typical incident occurred on January 4, 1894, when the life-boat went to the assistance of the *St. Alexil,* of Copenhagen, which had come to grief on the Buxey sands. The story is vividly described in the service record, from which the following is an extract.

"On reaching the wreck we could see the crew clinging to the deckhouse. Heavy seas were breaking over her and it was impossible to get near; so we made signs for the crew to attach something floatable to a rope, which they did, but it fouled the gear. We then sailed to windward, made for the wreck again and this time managed to throw the grappling into the rigging. Three of the crew then crawled out on the mast and we then threw a rope to them to make fast. . . . We were then able to haul the life-boat to the wreck so that the men could jump into the boat. The captain, however, was too weak to do so, and we had to throw him a rope, which he made fast about his body.

"As the coxswain was about to lift him into the boat he himself missed his foothold and fell overboard, sustaining a severe cut over the eye. But still having hold of the rope that was fast to the captain, the crew were able to haul him in, and then dragged the captain through the surf into the boat. We made for Clacton under close-reefed sails and arrived at the pier at 2.30 p.m. after a fearful journey. Both life-boat and men were covered in ice."

Nothing need be added to that simple yet graphic account except that the entire crew of the *St. Alexil*—seven men—were safely brought ashore.

Hurricane force

Five years later, in January 1899, when a really fierce gale was blowing, observers noticed that a ship—she turned out to be the *Hawkesdale*, bound from Hamburg to Melbourne—was aground on the Longsands and in danger of breaking up. The life-boat men were at once summoned and, though the wind was blowing at hurricane force, they launched the *Albert Edward II* and set out, close-reefed, for the scene of the disaster. Only after a long fight against the elemental forces of the sea did they succeed in getting alongside the stricken ship.

Eighteen men were taken off, and the life-boat was just about to leave for the return trip when someone remembered that the ship's cat had been left on board. Despite all the hazards involved, one of the *Hawkesdale's* crew insisted on clambering back to search for the missing animal, which everyone thought must be dead. However, it was found clinging to a mast and was rescued, little the

Elizabeth I visited St. Osyth's abbey twice—in 1561 and 1579. Reproduced by courtesy of the National Portrait Gallery.

St. Osyth's Priory. The topiary garden and the "abbot's tower," a place in which time stands still—despite the clock!

St. Osyth's Priory. Holm oak reputed to have been planted by Elizabeth I.

St. Osyth's Priory, near Clacton-on-Sea, is a "must" for visitors who love old, historic places. The great gateway, shown here, is one of its most admired features.

Brightlingsea. The Anchor hotel, standing practically at the water's edge.

Trinity Street, Colchester. On the right is the tower of Holy Trinity church, which dates back to the time of the Saxon kings. John Wilbye, the Elizabethan madrigalist, lies buried in the churchyard.

The Norman castle, now a scheduled monument, is occupied by the Colchester and Essex Museum, and contains the finest collection of Romano-British objects in the country.

Colchester. St. Botolph's priory, founded in 1106, was ruined during the siege of Colchester in 1648. The west front, shown here, is still ruggedly impressive. Most of the material used in its construction was of Roman origin.

Colchester, the old Siege House, built in the fifteenth century. It played a prominent part in the civil war and the woodwork is heavily pitted with bullet holes.

Frinton-on-Sea was first developed as a seaside resort by Sir Richard Powell Cooper in the 1890s. It has a spacious, gently shelving beach and miles of golden sands.

Frinton-on-Sea. The greensward, which fifty years ago was twice as wide as now, is one of the town's most attractive natural features.

Comarques, Thorpe-le-Soken, the Queen Anne mansion in which Arnold Bennett, the famous novelist, lived for eight years and which he hoped to make his home "for everlasting." It is surrounded by a fine and spacious garden.

worse for its adventure. Two of the *Albert Edward's* men, while holding on to the ropes at the side of the doomed vessel, had the flesh torn from the palms of their hands, and the coxswain suffered severe injuries when the tiller broke loose and struck him in the face. At last, after beating to windward all the way, the *Albert Edward* managed to deposit its cargo of shipwrecked mariners on storm-battered Clacton beach.

Again in 1891 there was drama when a man came ashore in an open boat with news that his ship, the schooner *Babel*, was wrecked on the Gunfleet sands. A Clacton poet, the late Mr. E. J. Clark, has described what happened in the following lines:

The life-boat's crew were summoned; in howling gale she sped,
And when she arrived at the scene of the wreck
Two men were found upon her, one of them almost dead.
Both were in the rigging, as the ship was breaking fast,
The others had all been swept away in the easterly blast.
One of the two survivors with the help of our crew was saved,
But the other, frozen to the mast, was beyond all human aid.
'Twas then that Jerry Roper, a member of our crew,
Climbed up that mast and cut him down, a gallant thing to do.
A lad of only nineteen, they bore him o'er the wave
To find his rest in the churchyard—in a humble sailor's grave.

These lines, quoted from a much longer narrative, were written by Mr. Clark, who was a member of the Clacton R.N.L.I. committee, for inclusion in a short history of the

Clacton life-boat—a project that unfortunately had to be abandoned.

Dunkirk

A great deal more could be recorded about such incidents, but something must now be said about later events. The third *Albert Edward*, a motorized craft, remained in service for the twenty years 1901-21, and was succeeded by temporary life-boats. The *Edward Z. Dresden*, launched in 1929, remained in commission until 1949, when the station again had to rely on a series of temporary boats. Clacton's present life-boat, housed on the pier and open to inspection by holiday visitors, is the *Sir Godfrey Baring*, purchased in 1952 from institution funds.

During World War II Clacton occupied a position of some strategic importance, for it was an obvious place for the enemy to attempt landings. One of the precautions taken was to blow up the middle of the pier, so that should invaders arrive they would find it useless for disembarkation purposes. This meant, of course, that the life-boat, housed at the end of the pier, had to be moved to another place. She was, in fact, taken to nearby Brightlingsea, berthed in the River Colne and kept afloat. The *Edward Z. Dresden*, it is interesting to recall, was one of the nineteen life-boats that sailed with the flotilla of " little ships " to Dunkirk in 1940 to help in the evacuation of the British expeditionary force and a number of French troops—337,000 men in all. Those were indeed momentous days.

Chapter VIII

COLCHESTER

The oldest inhabited town in Britain, with two thousand years of history behind it, can point to visually exciting relics of almost every bygone age.

FOR the antiquarian and the historian Colchester has for long been a happy hunting ground. This is understandable, for it has since time immemorial been a human settlement, a centre of successive civilizations in which the arts of both war and peace have flourished. It is also one of the most picturesque towns in Britain, with irresistible appeal for the photographer and artist.

Colchester, with a present population of 65,000, is only about an hour's journey from London by rail. Lying on the River Colne, it is a port and therefore accessible by boat. Anyone living in, or visiting, the nearby Essex coastal resorts can reach it without difficulty by motor car or bus. Transport facilities and roads are good throughout the area.

What to see

The visitor, whether coming from home or abroad, is almost invariably impressed on arriving in the town by the all-pervading atmosphere of antiquity. Everywhere are old, half-timbered houses, crumbling Roman and medieval walls, centuries-old churches and ancient inns. These may, of course, be found elsewhere—even in the heart of London—but nowhere in such abundance. There are, indeed, parts of Colchester that have all the appearance of a film set built at enormous cost as the background to an Elizabethan play.

A good starting point for a rapid exploration of the town is the castle—where, incidentally, a useful booklet entitled " What to see in Colchester " may be purchased for a few coppers. This not only contains a street plan, but outlines two suggested tours covering most of the places of major interest. Both can easily be done on foot during the course of a single day.

Just prior to the Christian era Colchester was the capital of the British chieftain Cunobelin (Shakespeare's Cymbeline), and though no ancient British buildings have survived the archæologists have unearthed plenty of pottery, coins and other small objects. Roman remains are to be seen in several different places. There are, for example, sections of the Roman wall, with projecting bastions, in Priory Street and on Balkerne Hill; and these, with their surroundings, have both architectural and historical interest. The Saxons have left their mark on Colchester, notably in the tower of Holy Trinity church, which dates back to the time of Edward the Confessor and incorporates brick and other material of Roman origin. All around Holy Trinity are narrow streets and lanes in which it is quite easy to get lost.

Only a few yards distant from the church is the famous house known as Tymperleys, in which the Elizabethan pioneer of electricity, Dr. William Gilberd, lived for many years. Quite near, too, are Scheregate Steps, in medieval times the site of an old gateway, and these can hardly fail to delight. A short walk from Scheregate Steps along Vineyard Street or Osborne Street brings one to the impressive ruins of St. Botolph's priory.

Colchester castle, besides being a good rallying centre for tourists, is well worth visiting, for it houses a collection of Romano-British treasure trove without equal in the country. Raised by William the Conqueror in 1880, the castle was at one time a truly formidable fortress, two stories higher than at present, and virtually impregnable until gunpowder was invented. Today only the keep or tower remains, but it has great strength and dignity. The castle, a scheduled monument, is the home of the Colchester and Essex Museum, and stands in a pleasant park. It is probable that the temple built by the emperor Claudius in commemoration of his victory over the Belgic defenders of Camulodunum occupied this identical site.

Outside the castle gates is the war memorial, designed by the sculptor H. C. Fehr and unveiled in 1923. Hollytrees, a fine old mansion, which is now corporation property, is in the same enclave, and dates back to the early Georgian era. This mansion, too, acts as a museum and may be visited—admission free.

The Siege House

Even today, perhaps, it may be truthfully said with Dr. Johnson that "there is nothing yet contrived by man which produces so much happiness as a good tavern or inn." Colchester is famous for its inns, and several of them are of great historical interest. There is, for example, the Marquess of Granby, on North Hill, which gives us an excellent idea of what sixteenth-century architecture was like. With its quaint front windows and ornamental carvings it is in many ways unique. Several other inns—among them the Red Lion and the George—are equally beguiling.

Stockwell Street, in the "old Dutch quarter," is also

worth a brief inspection. Here are several houses with projecting upper stories and crooked gables that were built while the Wars of the Roses were still being fought. Colchester was at one time a prosperous weaving town, and it was in these houses that the Dutch and Flemish weavers lived. Then there are the churches of Colchester, St. James's, St. Peter's, St. Martin's and several others, which give the town so much of its essential character.

During the civil war Colchester was on the side of King Charles and withstood a twelve-week siege by the Parliamentarian troops. Memories of that troubled period are preserved in the Siege House in East Street, the timbers of which are still riddled with bullet holes.

A landmark

Though proud of its 2,000 years of history, Colchester is by no means buried in the past—quite the reverse, as a walk along the lively High Street will quickly prove. Here, among the old churches and inns, are modern supermarkets, banks, television and radio shops, newsagents, offices of solicitors and chartered accountants, restaurants and cafés. Colchester also has its industries, ranging from rose-growing to the manufacture of diesel engines (to say nothing of the oyster fishery).

Finally there is the Town Hall, built in 1899 to supersede an earlier building. Statues of local celebrities—including Queen Boadicea, William Gilberd and Eudo Dapifer (steward to William II)—adorn its main front. Standing on the site of the Norman moot hall, it is a quite remarkable example of municipal architecture. Its elegant tower, crowned by a figure of St. Helena and 162 feet high, is a Colchester landmark visible for miles around.

Chapter IX

FRINTON-ON-SEA

Youngest—and most decorous—of the Essex seaside resorts.

SITUATED on a secluded part of the coast between Clacton and Walton, Frinton-on-Sea lacks many, indeed most, of the things that the average man and his family expect to find in a seaside holiday resort. Frinton has no pier, no scenic railway, no Kursaal, no cinema, no fun fairs, no holiday camps and no cockle stalls. It makes little provision for—in fact it severely frowns on—the overflowing coach parties, the day trippers who bring their picnic hampers with them, tramps, hoodlums, and owners of transistor radios. All these types, under some unwritten but well-understood law, are *verboten.*

Frinton, in fact, is uncompromisingly, even defiantly, "different." What we find on arrival is a town of tree-lined avenues, commodious villas, comfortable hotels, select boarding houses, high-class shops and well-behaved people. Its offerings in the way of natural amenity are little more than a long sea-lawn graced by a few clumps of wind-bent trees, a sandy beach, and the open sea. So there is bathing in Frinton and there is boating. There are also gardens, playing fields, the facilities for happy bucket-and-spade holidays and—let it be gratefully recorded—the conditions for enjoying a little peace and quiet.

Development

Our overall impression on leaving the station or bus stop is of a wholly modern town owing little if anything to the past. That impression, however, is not altogether correct. Frinton is mentioned in Domesday, and so may look back on over 900 years of history. The church of St. Mary the Virgin, one of the smallest places of worship in the country, belongs to the late fourteenth century. However, old Frinton, including the two manors of Frietuna and Frientuna, has largely vanished, for here, as at Walton, a continuous process of erosion has been at work, and whatever there was of Saxon or Norman Frinton has long since fallen over the cliffs and been swallowed up by the sea.

On the whole, therefore, it is true to say that Frinton is the youngest as well as the most decorous of the Essex seaside resorts. Much of the careful planning immediately evident is attributable to the foresight of Sir Richard Powell Cooper, who late in the nineteenth century owned the sea-front. However, it was only after 1903, when his property was acquired by the urban district council, that Frinton began to assume its present shape and character. A sea wall, a breakwater and thirty-two timber groins on the foreshore were constructed as part of a scheme to strengthen the sea defences. Later, when the esplanade and greensward had been completed, discerning London families recognized its attractions as a retreat "far from the madding crowd," in which the annual holiday could be enjoyed.

Frinton's growth was, however, kept within well-defined bounds—even today the resident population is only 4,000—and the "garden suburb" atmosphere has been carefully preserved.

Surroundings

The greater part of the town lies in a triangle of land between the railway line and the sea. Captious critics often remark that some of the famous avenues have been a little too grandiosely named: First Avenue, Second Avenue, right up to Fifth Avenue; and there is a hint—dare one suggest it?—of varsity and old-school-tie exclusiveness in the naming of some roads: Cambridge Road, Oxford Road, Eton Road, Winchester Road, and so on. The claim, so proudly made, that Connaught Avenue (opened by the Duchess of Connaught in 1904) is the " Bond Street of East Anglia " may also, perhaps, be regarded as evidence of the town's preoccupation with questions of social status, quality and *bon ton*.

Though there is a marked tendency for Frinton to " keep itself to itself," and to resent plebeian intrusion, it does offer good facilities to those of its guests who become restive and want to venture over the border—i.e. the level crossing—into the world beyond. Indeed, as a centre from which to explore north Essex and south Suffolk the choice of Frinton could hardly be bettered. Dedham, East Bergholt, Flatford mill, in fact the whole of the Constable country, Manningtree, Mistley, Harwich and Dovercourt are all easily reached by car. For the walkers there are footpaths over the cliffs to Great Holland and Walton-on-the-Naze, and lanes that lead to silvery backwaters and sleepy, half-forgotten villages in the hinterland.

There are for example the " Sokens "—i.e. districts that were formerly under special jurisdiction. How they originated is quite a story in itself, but briefly they were assigned to the dean and chapter of the first St. Paul's, London, by Eadulf, a Saxon thane, and after A.D. 941 became subject to the ecclesiastical authority. One of the three estates was Walton-le-Soken—now Walton-on-the-Naze—and over a stall in the present cathedral building may be seen an inscription in Latin which records that Walton church and the land surrounding it were " overwhelmed by the sea." Both Kirby-le-Soken and Thorpe-le-Soken are worth visiting for their churches. The latter is also noteworthy for its links with a major English novelist.

Arnold Bennett, author of *The Old Wives' Tale* and many another enthralling saga of the " five towns," came to live in Thorpe-le-Soken in 1913, when his reputation was at its peak, and lived there for eight years. He had purchased Comarques, a stately Queen Anne mansion surrounded by fourteen acres of ground, and intended to make it his home " for everlasting," but fate willed otherwise and he was forced to change his plans. While at Comarques he wrote one novel with an Essex setting, *The Lion's Share*, but it does not quite achieve the authenticity of the stories that deal with the Potteries, of which he was a native.

Sports

Whatever Frinton's shortcomings in other respects may be it does look after the sports enthusiasts. There is not as yet a racecourse, but the horse-riders are well provided for; and the yachtsmen, with the Walton backwaters so close at hand, have nothing to complain about. South of the town, adjoining the sea wall, there is an eighteen-hole golf course, with plenty of hazards to challenge experienced players, and there is also a nine-hole course for juniors. There are cricket matches throughout the season; and in the Park Playing Fields and elsewhere are putting greens and facilities for bowls and croquet.

Nor must Frinton's passion for the ancient and aristocratic game of tennis be overlooked. In fact, its annual tennis tournaments enjoy considerable fame, and during tennis week, held in July, and while the junior tournament is on in August an intense Wimbledon atmosphere pervades the town from end to end. " The well-appointed tennis club," as a brochure issued by the council tells us, " has twenty-two grass courts and four hard courts, catering for all classes of player."

Note the democratic ring of that " all classes," with its implication that Frinton has been maligned and is by no means the aloof, dignified, genteel, superior, snooty place that its detractors have declared it to be, but on the contrary is friendly, genial, free-and-easy, sporty. Certainly for those a little tired of the hurly-burly of town life it can be very pleasant.

Chapter X

JOHN CONSTABLE

Easily reached from the coast by motor coach or car is the delightful countryside in north Essex and just across the border in Suffolk immortalized by England's greatest landscape painter.

THE River Stour, which flows into the sea at Harwich, is forty-seven miles long and forms the boundary between Suffolk and Essex for the greater part of that distance. Close to its banks, on the Suffolk side, lies East Bergholt, where in 1776 the greatest of all English landscape artists was born. On the Essex side of the stream we find the village of Dedham, and it was here that he received his education.

John Constable was the son of a miller who owned two windmills and two watermills in the district, and was by country standards a man of worth and substance. John, while still a scholar at Dedham grammar school, had made studies and sketches of the peaceful scenes near the paternal home, scenes which, as he himself was to admit, virtually forced him to become a landscape painter.

The Stour fascinated him, as did many other parts of Essex, particularly Maldon, Rochford, South End and Hadleigh; and evidence of this is to be found in many of his letters. " I was so delighted," he wrote in 1814," with the scenery as to forget that my mind had been so long a stranger to happiness." Certainly he had a deep emotional attachment to the area, on both sides of the river, which he was later to immortalize in many a noble canvas.

Leaving the grammar school at Dedham, Constable busied himself for a year or so in his father's mills, continuing, however, with his art studies, in which he was encouraged by Sir George Beaumont, who introduced him to the works of Claude, Girtin and other masters. In 1795 the young painter deserted his native village for a time, hopeful that in the great city of London he might be able, like Reynolds and Gainsborough before him, to set his foot on the road to fame and fortune. For several years, however, he remained in the struggling stage, alternating his life in the metropolis with extended stays in the country.

Not until 1799, when he was twenty-three, could he decide what his future life's work should be. In that year the Royal Academy received him as a student, and three years later it exhibited his first landscape. The prospect of becoming a flour-miller receded, and he began to rely on his brush to provided him with a livelihood.

Strangely enough, Constable embarked on his career as a portrait painter—landscapes, on which his heart was set and so obviously his bent from the very first, were not as yet a remunerative form of art. Mechanically, one feels, he painted faces, while all the time his thoughts were on the Stour, the lush meadows in which his father's mills were grinding corn, and the woodlands surrounding his old school.

The portraits, therefore, did not score any remarkable success, and it was with " Dedham Vale," a masterly landscape, that he first established his right to be considered a major artist. This famous painting first saw the light of day in 1811 when Constable was thirty-six. Composed on the summit of the church tower in Langham, it at once marked him out as a painter of great daring and originality. Landscapes so full of movement, so colourful and so natural were quite a new thing in those days. The more stolid members of the Royal Academy regarded the young man as a rebel and were none too pleased.

Langham church is, incidentally, no great distance from the " Glebe Farm " which figures in a number of Constable's oil paintings and sketches.

" The Haywain "

It was in the same year that " Dedham Vale " was painted that Constable's romance with Maria Bicknell began. They were in love but could not marry, partly because of parental objections and partly because of his prospects, which financially were far from settled. The reference to his " unhappiness " already quoted was not unconnected with this unfortunate state of affairs. However, the impediments were finally overcome and the two became man and wife in 1816. By that time Constable was turning from portrait painting and beginning to concentrate on the magnificent landscapes that have made him famous the world over.

" The Haywain," exhibited at the French salon in 1824, created quite a furore, and the exacting critics were unanimous in their praise. Admiration of Constable's work in England was less generous, for the artist, like the prophet, is often without honour in his own land, but works such as " Dedham Lock or the Leaping Horse," and " Flatford Mill on the River Stour " had their staunch adherents even then.

In 1819 Constable was elected an A.R.A., and at about the same time his financial affairs took a turn for the better. His wife inherited £8,000 from an uncle, and there is every evidence that this windfall enabled Constable to devote his full energies to landscape. He developed his amazing technique with great rapidity, often laying on colour with the knife instead of the brush and throwing overboard one accepted convention after another.

John Constable was indeed a born innovator, an artist whose whole outlook and method were regarded as vaguely revolutionary, certainly unorthodox. The virtues that we now so much admire in him were considered vices—he was too bold, too experimental, his break with tradition was too complete, for the liking of his fellow Academicians, who were frankly patronizing in their attitude. Still, in the end he triumphed, if only for the reason that his work had, and still has, an irresistible appeal for the many people who like the fields, the homely activities and the open skies of the country. These Constable depicted with a superb and incomparable skill.

There was in his case no need to turn to classical literature, no need to visit foreign lands, for inspiration. He found what he wanted close at hand. His province extended along the banks of the Stour, the stream that divides Suffolk from Essex and separates the artist's birthplace from his school.

Constable was in fact content to depict in one brilliant canvas after another the quiet beauty, the changing moods and the charm of what has since come to be known as the "Constable country."

Chapter XI

WALTON-ON-THE-NAZE

One of the great charms of the Essex coast is the variety of its holiday resorts, which cater for all tastes, all temperaments and all ages. There are noisy, brash places full of amusement arcades and pop-music; there are quiet, superior places where people read romantic novels and no louder sound is heard than that of the dinner gong. There are still other places, perhaps the best, that offer homely comfort without being either too boisterous or too exclusive. One such place, avoiding all extremes, is dealt with in the following pages.

AT first glance Walton-on-the-Naze, especially if one should happen to arrive on a rainy day, can be disappointing. There are no multi-story hotels, no penthouses, no waving palm trees or blossoming sub-tropical gardens. The street plan is frankly bewildering, the sea-front is a wilderness of concrete, and the pier, though it claims to be the second longest in the country, is hardly a thing of beauty. In such a mood of disenchantment Walton is apt to strike one as a case of arrested development and lost opportunities. The surroundings, too, appear to be rather flat and devoid of visual charm, while the sea looks a dull grey waste, very wet and uninviting.

Impressions of this kind are, however, quickly dispelled on closer acquaintance. There are good sands at Walton, the North Sea with the sun shining on it is pleasantly blue, and the breezes that whip the waves into a fine lacework of

Flatford mill, in the Constable country.

The sixteenth-century thatched cottage close to Flatford mill in the Constable country.

John Constable. Reproduced by courtesy of the National Portrait Gallery.

Walton-on-the-Naze and its implacable enemy. The encroaching sea is " taking a bite " at the land but with little effect, for the defences here are now exceptionally strong.

The sea is also Walton's good friend, for it attracts the crowds of holiday-makers and tourists.

Walton-on-the-Naze. Houses and gardens along the sea front. The bust commemorates a hero of World War I—Private G. Columbine, V.C., killed in action on March 22, 1918. The inscription reads : " He refused to retire when he might have done so, and by his self-sacrifice to duty was the means of holding up large numbers of the enemy for four hours."

Walton-on-the-Naze. An attractive group of thatched cottages. In Elizabethan days they were six miles from the sea, but coastal erosion has reduced the distance to a few hundred yards.

Walton-on-the-Naze pier, the second longest in the country.

Harwich, on the way to the harbour—old houses with symbols of modernity hoisted over the rooftops. The spire of St. Nicholas's church is in the background. "A pretty town," said Queen Elizabeth I of Harwich, "and lacks nothing."

Harwich—a busy harbour scene. During the Commonwealth and after the Restoration the town became an important naval base and has remained so ever since.

Harwich. A public garden, picturesque old houses and the spire of St. Nicholas's church, which was rebuilt in 1825 but contains, among other monuments belonging to the old church, a twelfth-century font.

Dovercourt is part of Harwich, acting as its residential centre. Here will be found a pleasant beach, a promenade giving fine views over the North Sea, a church, a statue of Queen Victoria (between the two shelters) and well-kept cliff gardens.

foam are healthy and invigorating, Looking round at the shops, the church, the older houses and the thatched cottages, one realizes that Walton, lacking perhaps in elegance and sophistication, has plenty of character.

The district, too, is interesting and worth exploring, for it contains many a picturesque nook and bears evidence of having been inhabited by man for thousands of years. On the jutting promontory of the Naze, where the Trinity House tower now stands, primitive men had a settlement, for vast quantities of Neolithic stone implements—arrow-heads, axe-heads and spear-heads—have been found there.

Walton's famous Red Crag has yielded up even more astonishing treasures—elephant and rhinoceros bones and the fossil remains of species long extinct. The Romans probably knew Walton—indeed, if we may believe Morant and other historians they built the wall from which its name is derived (Walton=wall town). In the backwaters, a uniquely attractive feature, Saxons and Danes fought life-and-death battles. Later came the Norman conquerors to impose their rule on the marshland villages.

More persistent, more relentless, however, than any of these human invaders rolling in successive waves across the countryside has been a natural enemy—the sea.

Coastal erosion

The reasons for this have already been indicated. Much of the land in and around Walton is low-lying; the cliffs, because of their porous nature, are continually crumbling, and over the centuries there have been innumerable land-slides and subsidences of the soil. In many places where this happened the sea advanced relentlessly inland, through simple operation of the law of gravity. Even in Roman times there was this problem of coastal erosion, for it is believed that the Roman wall was demolished by storms and swirling tides. This wall, incidentally, was probably a rampart, or dyke, built up to keep back the water—a part of the sea defences and not a city wall in the usual sense.

The extent of the North Sea encroachment can be fully appreciated only when it is remembered that old Walton, as it was in medieval and even later times, now lies fathoms deep in the sea bed, silted up with sand, fragments of it visible from time to time when the tide recedes far enough. There was a parish church dating back to the thirteenth century—a small, towerless building, according to the surviving accounts of it, which gradually fell into a state of decay. Towards the end of the eighteenth century all that remained was the porch, in which the last wedding ceremony was performed just prior to the sea's final victory.

The erosion has not, of course, been allowed to go on entirely unrestricted. As far back as Stuart times experienced Dutch engineers were engaged at Walton and in the backwaters, building up the defences and reclaiming flooded land wherever possible. As recently as 1890 an Act of Parliament was passed giving the local board of commissioners authority to strengthen and extend the defences.

To some extent these works, carried out at heavy cost, have been successful—though they are still subject to fierce batterings. For example, on the night of January 31, 1953, a high tide, assisted by the wind, broke through and brought the low-lying parts of the town to the verge of disaster. Houses, caravans and schools were flooded to a depth of up to ten feet. Though no lives were lost many people were rendered homeless, at least temporarily, and it was months before the breach in the sea wall could be repaired and normal conditions were restored.

The sea is undoubtedly still Walton's worst enemy, attacking the coastline—now with brutal force, now with insidious guile—year in and year out; but, paradoxically, the sea is also Walton's best friend, for it brings the crowds of summer visitors.

A fashionable watering place

Two hundred years have now passed since medical men first advocated sea-bathing as a remedy for almost every ailment under the sun. Prior to about 1750 total immersion in water, whether hot or cold, was a rare occurrence in people's lives. Even washing the hands and face was a practice not indulged in too frequently, for excessive ablutions, it was believed, removed the natural oils from the skin and were therefore dangerous. Quite suddenly these ideas were abandoned, and everyone who could afford to do so made for the coast, there to wallow in salt water and even to drink it in small quantities, as if it were wine or an elixir! Royalty itself, in the person of George III, was caught up in the frenzy. There are amusing accounts of him being taken down to the water's edge in a high-wheeled bathing machine, with the flags flying, the band playing, and the crowds cheering as he took the plunge!

Walton seems to have attracted its first visitors during the Regency period. By the time that young Queen Victoria was on the throne the town had acquired its reputation as a watering place for people of quality in search of health and relaxation. Since the population of the town was then under 500, and the only way of maintaining communication with the outside world was by horse-drawn coach, it must have been very quiet there. Railways and steamboats were at the time still in their infancy, and the motor-car and aeroplane no more than dreams in the minds of half-crazy inventors.

A directory of Walton-on-the-Naze printed in 1839 gave a list of recommended boarding houses, or " lodgings " as they were then called. For the really genteel family, with plenty of money to spend and a retinue of servants, there was the Porta Bella hotel, " excellently well conducted," and no doubt provided with all the amenities then available. The stately terrace known as Navarino (named after a famous naval battle fought in 1827) dates back to this period.

Visitors, then as now, came to Walton for the bathing, for the sea air, and for a glimpse of tide-washed sands, of fishermen and sailing boats, of cormorants and gulls. They made expeditions to the Naze tower, and had picnic parties in the flower-spangled grass. They admired the views across the wide expanse of sea to the Suffolk coast, or wandered about at the foot of the cliffs looking for flint arrow-heads or other souvenirs of prehistoric man, just as we do today.

Annual regatta

Gentlemen with a commercial turn of mind will no doubt have interested themselves in the local " copperas house," which still flourished. (" Copperas," found in abundance at Walton, is a chemical substance of bluish-green colour used in the dying and tanning trades.) Others, more adventurously inclined, will have led expeditions into the surrounding countryside to inspect the windmills, the tidal mill and the martello tower built in 1804 and later used to house French prisoners. For the ladies, one imagines, there were dancing lessons, pianoforte playing and ritual afternoon teas. Everyone must have enjoyed the annual regatta.

Despite its troubled love-hate relationship with the sea, Walton has inevitably grown and expanded over the years, but not at the alarming rate that some other Essex resorts have done. The permanent population is still only approximately 3,000, and so it remains little more than a village—compact, homely and quiet.

Chapter XII

HISTORIC HARWICH AND DOVERCOURT

"*A pretty town,*" *said Queen Elizabeth I of Harwich,* "*and lacks nothing.*"

THE historian Thomas Wright, whose *History of Essex* has already been quoted, described the ancient and land-locked harbour of Harwich as " occupying a narrow point of land at the north-eastern extremity of Tendring hundred and of the county." To the south of the town, he goes on to say, is a cliff, constantly giving way to the action of the sea. This cliff, some fifty feet high, covered many acres of land, and at the bottom of it was a stratum of a peculiar kind of clay which on being exposed to the air hardened into a stone of sufficient durability to be used for the paving of streets. From the top of Beacon Cliff, as it was called, one could see " the higher parts of the town," with the two lighthouses, the handsome new church lately erected, and other public buildings." There was also a fine prospect of the shipping—both in the harbour and out at sea.

The description, though nearly 140 years have passed since it was penned, remains clearly recognizable, The fact is that Harwich, though as modern and well-equipped as any port in the country, still retains much of its original appearance and character. Of course, the big ocean-going steamships, the ferries, the motor traffic and many other things are unmistakably of the present century, but the crooked streets, the tumbledown but picturesque houses, the weatherbeaten inns and the quays clearly belong to an era that is past.

Little imagination is required to conjure up visions of tall-masted sailing ships riding at anchor in the harbour and jolly jack-tars making the most of a few hours ashore.

Ancient record

That Harwich should have risen to eminence as a haven for ships was a thing predestined by nature, for here at the confluence of the Orwell and Stour is a pool of protected deep water as inviting to a mariner as anywhere on England's east coast. Even the Saxons and Danes knew this; in fact the earliest recorded event of importance in the history of Harwich is the great sea battle fought in 885 between Danish and Saxon fleets. This early struggle for the mouth of the Stour, which according to the *Anglo-Saxon Chronicle* resulted in an English victory, is proof that both invaders and defenders appreciated that the position had high strategic value.

There is no mention of Harwich in the Domesday survey, but a later record, dated 1270, mentions it as a small village belonging to the manor of Dovercourt, and of little consequence. Fifty years later it was a borough and market town in its own right, Edward II having, at the request of his brother, Thomas de Brotherton, granted it a charter. After 1319, therefore, Harwich began to establish itself as a separate entity. The town's privileges as a free borough were confirmed by later monarchs—notably by Elizabeth I and James I, who restored to Harwich the right, dormant since the reign of Edward III, to return two members to Parliament, and sanctioned the holding of two weekly markets—on Tuesdays and Fridays—and two annual fairs.

Commerce

The year 1543 stands out in the annals of early Harwich because of the visit paid to it by Henry VIII to inspect ships of the Navy then assembled in the harbour. In the following century, when it was a major base for fighting the Dutch, Charles II hurried to the town to direct the strengthening of its defences. It was on his orders that shallow-draught sloops were built, capable of sailing over the sands in the harbour and engaging the Dutch picaroons, or pirates, then harassing the coast. The naval engagement of 1666 between the Dutch and English fleets drew many Harwich men to the top of Beacon Hill, from which the action was clearly visible. Two lighthouses, with a new type of lamp, were erected at about this time and replaced the " blazing fire and six candles " that had previously served as a warning to ships at sea.

The trading prosperity of Harwich was in medieval times largely based on the exchange of commodities such as wool and wheat between this country and Flanders, and at a later period on the Post Office mail packets. " Four packets sailed every week for Göttingen," recorded Wright, "and this [Harwich] was a principal place of embarkation for Holland and Germany, but this source of emolument has since been diminished or destroyed by the establishment of steam packets."

The town was indeed gravely affected when the mails to the Continent were diverted to other and presumably more convenient routes. Disappointed in their hopes of a restoration of the mail-packet services via Harwich, the inhabitants turned to other maritime pursuits, in particular North Sea fishing and shipbuilding. Those with a taste for adventure and law-breaking joined the ranks of the smugglers who were active all along the coast. According to legend, they kept half the town cellars filled with contraband goods.

Harwich today is again a busy port, handling thousands of tons of imported and exported goods. Passenger ships leave Parkeston Quay regularly for the Hook of Holland, Antwerp and Esbjerg; and in the summer months there are sailings to Zeebrugge, Göteborg and other continental ports. Harwich continues to be, as it was in the past, an important naval base.

An old town

While the fascination of the quays and harbour is irresistible there is much else of compelling interest to be seen. The redoubt, or martello tower—which has walls eight feet thick and formerly bristled with guns mounted on a revolving platform—was one of the largest of those reputedly impregnable fortresses ever built. It dates back to the Napoleonic wars, when an invasion of Essex was expected almost daily.

Now, as then, Harwich has three main streets, High Street, West Street and Church Street, with interesting lanes and alleys branching off on either side. Here the visitor in search of antiquity and romance will find enough to engross him for hours on end. Apart from the principal buildings, such as the Town Hall (formerly the Great Eastern hotel) and the Customs House, there are groups of half-timbered houses and several inns of historic interest. One of them, the Three Cups, has associations with Sir Francis Drake and other famous men who went down to the sea in ships.

Towering over the roofs of the town is the steeple of St. Nicholas, the " handsome new church " of which Wright speaks. Raised on the site of a much older building, its interior contains, among other things, a twelfth-century font. Christopher Jones, master of the *Mayflower*, which took the Pilgrim Fathers to America, was married in this church.

Dovercourt

As we have seen, Harwich was at one time a mere appendage of Dovercourt; now their positions are reversed—Dovercourt is part of Harwich, acting as its residential quarter and weekend playground. Here will be found a pleasant beach, an esplanade giving fine views over the North Sea, a church, a statue of Queen Victoria, and a good shopping centre. Add to these amenities the fact that Dovercourt, though on the east coast, faces due south, and it is easy to see why it has achieved such popularity as a seaside resort of the quieter and more restful kind.

Chapter XIII

CAPTAINS COURAGEOUS

Before actually saying goodbye to the Essex coast at least one rollicking tale of the past deserves to be told—that of the Harwich shipmaster Thomas Thompson and the capture, in 1592, of the Madre de Dios, *a great Spanish treasure ship.*

THOUGH it can boast no early circumnavigators of the globe, Essex in its time has produced some truly remarkable seafarers. There was for example Robert Moore, of Harwich, who played the leading part in an action against a Turkish galley and was instrumental in freeing 266 Christian slaves from their servitude. All England in 1579 resounded with his praise.

Another seaman of nation-wide renown was the Harwich shipmaster Thomas Thompson, who rose to be one of the six " principal masters of the Navy "—a position of high responsibility. There was a dash of the pirate in his make-up, however, and the greatest moment of his career came in 1592 when he sailed into Harwich harbour in a vessel owned by Sir John Hawkins—the *Dainty*—with her holds full of Spanish treasure. Skipper and crew paraded the streets with their spoils, and the day, with its auction sales, tavern brawls and singing of sea shanties, was remembered for decades after.

Enumerated among the shipmasters of Harwich in 1582, six years prior to the sailing of the great Armada, were John and Thomas Gray, who acted as the captains of small but highly combative fighting ships. John in fact rose to be master of the *Revenge*, Drake's flagship in 1588, though he had flown the Jolly Roger at an earlier stage of his career. There had actually been a warrant out against him in 1567 for piracy. Thomas Gray was master of the *Ark Royal*, flagship of the fleet in Armada year.

The " great carrack "

About the daring sea-dogs Edward Musgrave and Roger, John and Henry Hankyn many a stirring tale could be told. John Hankyn was a member of the commission of inquiry which in Elizabethan times was appointed to investigate the alleged deterioration of Harwich harbour. Son of an Icelandic fishing-boat commander, John took part in numerous expeditions against Spain, always acquitting himself with honour.

His kinsman, Roger Hankyn, commanded Raleigh's flagship in the Cadiz voyage of 1596 and a few years later was sailing the seas as master of an armed merchantman. He also performed useful work in training aristocratic " landlubbers "—gentlemen of the court who were the nominal captains of line-of-battle ships—into sailormen of repute.

The capture of the great Spanish treasure ship *Madre de Dios* is inseparably associated with the name of another Harwich shipmaster, Christopher Newport, a man of dominating personality who in 1591-2 sailed to the West Indies in command of an expedition consisting of the *Golden Dragon* and three other vessels. He visited Hispaniola, Cuba, Honduras and Florida, sacked their principal cities and either captured or destroyed a score of Spanish ships.

It was following these exploits on the voyage home that

he hailed Sir John Burgh, a friend of Raleigh, and assisted in the attack on the *Madre de Dios*—the " great carrack " as she was called. The action against her began at Flores, in the Azores, on August 3, 1592, and lasted sixteen hours. When, at the end of a stubborn fight, she was boarded the English sailors were astounded by the fabulous riches she carried. Stowed away in her capacious holds was a cargo estimated to be worth £250,000 in terms of Elizabethan currency.

Reckless plunder by the English officers and crews reduced this total by one half and the remainder became, as was perhaps only to be expected, the subject of bitter dispute. The victorious fleet returned to England in safety, but torn by dissensions, and the commander, Burgh, becoming involved in a quarrel over division of the booty, was challenged to fight a duel, in which he lost his life.

Returning, however, to the *Madre de Dios*, it was Christopher Newport, most famous of the Harwich ship-masters, who took command of her on the homeward voyage. He brought his prize safely into Dartmouth harbour on September 7, 1592, and from the Devon port sailed in Hawkins's ship the *Dainty* for Harwich, bearing with him his own share of the plunder, much of which was sold in the streets of the town, as already related.

Sea fever

He did not, however, retire and settle down quietly in the Essex countryside as he might have done. The sea was in his blood and he was soon embarked on even more adventurous voyages. During the reign of James I, Christopher Newport was placed in sole charge of the Virginia expedition. Second and third voyages followed in 1607-8 and a fourth in 1609, when, as a shipmate of Sir John Somers, he was cast ashore during a storm on the " Devil Islands," which Shakespeare may possibly have had in mind when writing *The Tempest*, in the first act of which occurs the line " Now would I give a thousand furlongs of sea for an acre of barren land."

The islands were actually the Bermudas and must have been visited by Europeans earlier, for they were overrun by wild hogs. Since that day of storm and shipwreck in 1609 the Bermudas have remained a British possession.

Altogether five voyages were made by Christopher Newport to the new world, and still the roving spirit, the sea fever, burnt in him as strongly as ever. In 1612 he entered the service of the East India Company and was entrusted by its directors with command of three expeditions—to Persia, to the mouth of the Indus, and to the East Indian spice islands.

These were remarkable and successful voyages, undertaken in small wooden ships with few amenities on board and only the roughest charts and navigational aids. Newport himself was made of iron, his one love being " the wheel's kick, and wind's song, and the white sails shaking." He died in 1617 at Batum, after a life packed full of romance and adventure.